Mom, Dad, Tara, Tessa, and Tim are eating breakfast. They live on a beautiful island. Every day is sunny there.

Tara is fishing. Tim and Tessa are playing in the ocean.

We can go to Parrot Island in our boat!

Tim and Tessa get in the boat.

Look at the beautiful parrots!

Hello, hello.

And, they're smart. They can talk!

4

The children are excited, but suddenly, the boat stops.

Oh, no! Look at the boat!

Quickly, swim to the island.

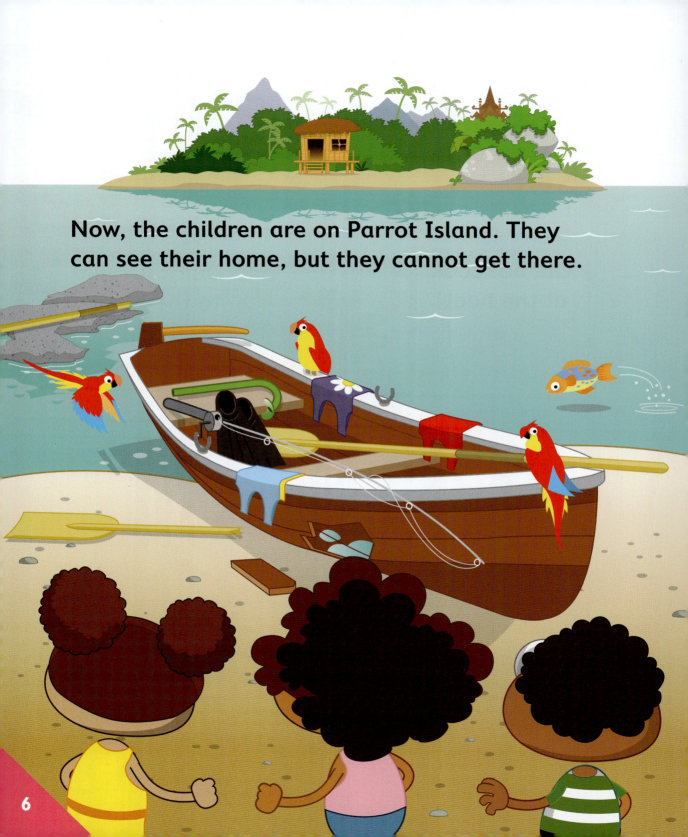

Now, the children are on Parrot Island. They can see their home, but they cannot get there.

The children walk down the beach.
They find a cave and go in.

7

The children see some monkeys in the trees.
The monkeys are playing with coconuts.

I've an idea.
Take a coconut!

The children see some parrots.
The parrots are playing with vines.

I've an idea! Take a parrot and some vines!

Then, the children see an old, empty house. They go in.

I can use this!

And, we can use these!

The children go back to the beach with the coconuts, the vines, the parrots, and the things from the house.

Activities

Before You Read

1 **Match the words and pictures.**

1 children   **2** animals   **3** boat   **4** island

After You Read

1 **Read and say *Yes* or *No*.**
  a The children live on Parrot Island.
  b The children see a picture in the cave.
  c The children make a boat.
  d The monkeys are smart.
  e Mom and Dad are angry.

2 **How do the children make their boat? What do they use?**
Read and circle.

parrots monkeys fish vines trees coconuts flashlight

Pearson Education Limited
Edinburgh Gate, Harlow,
Essex CM20 2JE, England
and Associated Companies throughout the world.

ISBN: 978-1-4479-7997-5

This edition first published by Pearson Education Ltd 2014

7 9 10 8 6

Text copyright © Pearson Education Ltd 2014

The moral rights of the author have been asserted
in accordance with the Copyright Designs and Patents Act 1988

Set in 19/23pt OT Fiendstar Semibold
Printed in China
SWTC/06

Illustrations: Stuart Trotter

For a complete list of the titles available in the Poptropica English Readers series please go to
www.pearsonelt.com/ourdiscoveryisland. Alternatively, write to your local Pearson Education office or to:
Pearson Readers Marketing Department, Pearson Education, Edinburgh Gate, Harlow, Essex CM20 2JE, England.